Poems of Emily Bro
Collection

Edited by

Debbie Brewer

Front cover image:

Portrait of Emily Bronte, by Patrick Branwell Bronte, 1833, held at the National Portrait Gallery.

Back cover image:

Part of the portrait of the Bronte sisters, by Patrick Branwell Bronte, 1834, held at the National Portrait Gallery

Copyright © 2019 Debbie Brewer

First published in July 2019 by Lulu.com

Distributed by Lulu.com

All rights reserved. No part of this book may be reproduced by any mechanical, photographic, or electronic process, or in the form of a phonographic recording. Nor may it be stored in a retrieval system, transmitted or otherwise be copied for public or private use, other than for fair use as brief quotations embodied in articles and reviews, without prior written permission of the author.

ISBN-13: 978-0-244-20000-8

First Edition

Poems Of Emily Bronte

A
Classic
Collection
Book

Poems of Emily Bronte

The Elder's Rebuke

The Lady To Her Guitar

The Wanderer From The Fold

Silent Is The House

R. Alcona To J. Brenzaida

Well Hast Thou Spoke

High Waving Heather, 'Neath Stormy Blasts Bending

Riches I Hold In Light

A Day Dream

To Imagination

Death, That Struck When I Was Most Confiding

The Two Children; Part 1 & Part 2

How Beautiful The Earth Is Still

The Prisoner. A Fragment

The Visionary

No Coward Soul Is Mine

Often Rebuked, Yet Always Back Returning

I Am The Only Being Whose Doom

A Little While, A Little While

Love And Friendship

Fall Leaves Fall

My Comforter

A Death – Scene

A Little Budding Rose

Anticipation

At Castle Wood

The Philosopher

The Sun Has Set

How Clear She Shines

Honours Martyr

Self-Interrogation

How Still, How Happy!

The Blue Bell

Come Hither, Child

Death!

Faith And Despondency

Far Away Is Mirth Withdrawn

Hope

I See Around Me Tombstones Grey

If Grief For Grief Can Touch Three

Last Lines

Me Thinks This Heart

Mild The Mist Upon The Hill

Moonlight Summer Moonlight

My Ladys Grave

Night Is Darkening Around Me

Oh For The Time When I Shall Sleep

Plead For Me

Remembrance

Shall Earth No More Inspire Thee

She Dried Her Tears

Song

Speak God Of Visions

Stanza

Stanzas

Stars

Sympathy

That Wind I Used To Hear It Swelling

The Night – Wind

The Old Stoic

The Prisoner

Wind Was Rough Which Tore

Yes, Holy Be Thy Resting Place

Oh, Thy Bright Eyes Must Answer Now

Warning And Reply

Loud Without The Wind Was Roaring

Encouragement

Shall Earth No More Inspire Thee

Far Far Away Is Mirth Withdrawn

Long Neglect Has Worn Away

Spellbound

Ah! Why, Because The Dazzling Sun

The Elder's Rebuke

'Listen! When your hair, like mine,
Takes a tint of silver grey;
When your eyes, with dimmer shine,
Watch life's bubbles float away:

When you, young man, have borne like me
The weary weight of sixty-three,
Then shall penance sore be paid
For those hours so wildly squandered;

And the words that now fall dead
On your ear, be deeply pondered—
Pondered and approved at last:
But their virtue will be past!

'Glorious is the prize of Duty,
Though she be 'a serious power';
Treacherous all the lures of Beauty,
Thorny bud and poisonous flower!

'Mirth is but a mad beguiling
Of the golden-gifted time;
Love—a demon-meteor, wiling
Heedless feet to gulfs of crime.

'Those who follow earthly pleasure,
Heavenly knowledge will not lead;
Wisdom hides from them her treasure,
Virtue bids them evil-speed!

'Vainly may their hearts repenting.
Seek for aid in future years;
Wisdom, scorned, knows no relenting;
Virtue is not won by fears.'

Thus spake the ice-blooded elder grey;
The young man scoffed as he turned away,
Turned to the call of a sweet lute's measure,
Waked by the lightsome touch of pleasure:
Had he ne'er met a gentler teacher,
Woe had been wrought by that pitiless preacher.

The Lady To Her Guitar

For him who struck thy foreign string,
I ween this heart has ceased to care;
Then why dost thou such feelings bring
To my sad spirit—old Guitar?

It is as if the warm sunlight
In some deep glen should lingering stay,
When clouds of storm, or shades of night,
Have wrapt the parent orb away.

It is as if the glassy brook
Should image still its willows fair,
Though years ago the woodman's stroke
Laid low in dust their Dryad-hair.

Even so, Guitar, thy magic tone
Hath moved the tear and waked the sigh;
Hath bid the ancient torrent moan,
Although its very source is dry.

The Wanderer From The Fold

How few, of all the hearts that loved,
Are grieving for thee now;
And why should mine to-night be moved
With such a sense of woe?

Too often thus, when left alone,
Where none my thoughts can see,
Comes back a word, a passing tone
From thy strange history.

Sometimes I seem to see thee rise,
A glorious child again;
All virtues beaming from thine eyes
That ever honoured men:

Courage and truth, a generous breast
Where sinless sunshine lay:
A being whose very presence blest
Like gladsome summer-day.

O, fairly spread thy early sail,
And fresh, and pure, and free,
Was the first impulse of the gale
Which urged life's wave for thee!

Why did the pilot, too confiding,
Dream o'er that ocean's foam,
And trust in Pleasure's careless guiding
To bring his vessel home?

For well he knew what dangers frowned,
What mists would gather, dim;
What rocks and shelves, and sands lay round
Between his port and him.

The very brightness of the sun
The splendour of the main,
The wind which bore him wildly on
Should not have warned in vain.

An anxious gazer from the shore—
I marked the whitening wave,
And wept above thy fate the more
Because—I could not save.

It wrecks not now, when all is over:
But yet my heart will be
A mourner still, though friend and lover
Have both forgotten thee!

Silent Is The House

Come, the wind may never again
Blow as now it blows for us;
And the stars may never again shine as now they shine;
Long before October returns,
Seas of blood will have parted us;
And you must crush the love in your heart, and I the love in mine!

R. Alcona To J. Brenzaida

Cold in the earth, and the deep snow piled above thee!
Far, far removed, cold in the dreary grave!
Have I forgot, my Only Love, to love thee,
Severed at last by Time's all-wearing wave?

Now, when alone, do my thoughts no longer hover
Over the mountains on Angora's shore;
Resting their wings where heath and fern-leaves cover
That noble heart for ever, ever more?

Cold in the earth, and fifteen wild Decembers
From those brown hills have melted into spring--
Faithful indeed is the spirit that remembers
After such years of change and suffering!

Sweet Love of youth, forgive if I forget thee
While the World's tide is bearing me along:
Sterner desires and darker hopes beset me,
Hopes which obscure but cannot do thee wrong.

No other Sun has lightened up my heaven;
No other Star has ever shone for me:
All my life's bliss from thy dear life was given
All my life's bliss is in the grave with thee.

But when the days of golden dreams had perished
And even Despair was powerless to destroy,
Then did I learn how existence could be cherished,
Strengthened and fed without the aid of joy;

Then did I check the tears of useless passion,
Weaned my young soul from yearning after thine;
Sternly denied its burning wish to hasten
Down to that tomb already more than mine!

And even yet, I dare not let it languish,
Dare not indulge in Memory's rapturous pain;
Once drinking deep of that divinest anguish,
How could I seek the empty world again?

Well Hast Thou Spoke

Well hast thou spoken, and yet not taught
A feeling strange or new;
Thou hast but roused a latent thought,
A cloud-closed beam of sunshine brought
To gleam in open view.

Deep down, concealed within my soul,
That light lies hid from men;
Yet glows unquenched--though shadows roll,
Its gentle ray cannot control--
About the sullen den.

Was I not vexed, in these gloomy ways
To walk alone so long?
Around me, wretches uttering praise,
Or howling o'er their hopeless days,
And each with Frenzy's tongue;--

A brotherhood of misery,
Their smiles as sad as sighs;
Whose madness daily maddened me,
Distorting into agony
The bliss before my eyes!

So stood I, in Heaven's glorious sun,
And in the glare of Hell;
My spirit drank a mingled tone,
Of seraph's song, and demon's moan;
What my soul bore, my soul alone
Within itself may tell!

Like a soft, air above a sea,
Tossed by the tempest's stir;
A thaw-wind, melting quietly
The snow-drift on some wintry lea;
No: what sweet thing resembles thee,
My thoughtful Comforter?

And yet a little longer speak,
Calm this resentful mood;
And while the savage heart grows meek,
For other token do not seek,
But let the tear upon my cheek
Evince my gratitude!

High Waving Heather, 'Neath Stormy Blasts Bending

High waving heather, 'neath stormy blasts bending,
Midnight and moonlight and bright shining stars;
Darkness and glory rejoicingly blending,
Earth rising to heaven and heaven descending,
Man's spirit away from its drear dungeon sending,
Bursting the fetters and breaking the bars.

All down the mountain sides, wild forest lending
One mighty voice to the life-giving wind;
Rivers their banks in the jubilee rending,
Fast through the valleys a reckless course wending,
Wider and deeper their waters extending,
Leaving a desolate desert behind.

Shining and lowering and swelling and dying,
Changing for ever from midnight to noon;
Roaring like thunder, like soft music sighing,
Shadows on shadows advancing and flying,
Lightning-bright flashes the deep gloom defying,
Coming as swiftly and fading as soon.

Riches I Hold In Light

Riches I hold in light esteem
And Love I laugh to scorn
And lust of Fame was but a dream
That vanished with the morn—

And if I pray, the only prayer
That moves my lips for me
Is – "Leave the heart that now I bear
And give me liberty."

Yes, as my swift days near their goal
'Tis all that I implore
Through life and death, a chainless soul
With courage to endure!

A Day Dream

On a sunny brae alone I lay
One summer afternoon;
It was the marriage-time of May
With her young lover, June.

From her Mother's heart seemed loath to part
That queen of bridal charms,
But her Father smiled on the fairest child
He ever held in his arms.

The trees did wave their plumy crests,
The glad birds carolled clear;
And I, of all the wedding guests,
Was only sullen there.

There was not one but wished to shun
My aspect void of cheer;
The very grey rocks, looking on,
Asked, "What do you do here?"

And I could utter no reply:
In sooth I did not know
Why I had brought a clouded eye
To greet the general glow.

So, resting on a heathy bank,
I took my heart to me;
And we together sadly sank
Into a reverie.

We thought, "When winter comes again
Where will these bright things be?
All vanished, like a vision vain,
An unreal mockery!

"The birds that now so blithely sing,
Through deserts frozen dry,
Poor spectres of the perished Spring
In famished troops will fly.

"And why should we be glad at all?
The leaf is hardly green,
Before a token of the fall
Is on its surface seen."

Now whether it were really so
I never could be sure-,
But as, in fit of peevish woe,
I stretched me on the moor,

A thousand thousand glancing fires
Seemed kindling in the air;
A thousand thousand silvery lyres
Resounded far and near:

Methought the very breath I breathed
Was full of sparks divine,
And all my heather-couch was wreathed
By that celestial shine.

And while the wide Earth echoing rang
To their strange minstrelsy,
The little glittering spirits sang,
Or seemed to sing, to me:

"O mortal, mortal, let them die;
Let Time and Tears destroy,
That we may overflow the sky
With universal joy.

"Let Grief distract the sufferer's breast,
And Night obscure his way;
They hasten him to endless rest,
And everlasting day.

"To Thee the world is like a tomb,
A desert's naked shore;
To us, in unimagined bloom,
It brightens more and more.

"And could we lift the veil and give
One brief glimpse to thine eye
Thou would'st rejoice for those that live,
Because they live to die."

The music ceased-the noonday Dream
Like dream of night withdrew
But Fancy still will sometimes deem
Her fond creation true.

To Imagination

When weary with the long day's care,
And earthly change from pain to pain,
And lost, and ready to despair,
Thy kind voice calls me back again
O my true friend, I am not lone
While thou canst speak with such a tone!

So hopeless is the world without,
The world within I doubly prize;
Thy world where guile and hate and doubt
And cold suspicion never rise;
Where thou and I and Liberty
Have undisputed sovereignty.

What matters it that all around
Danger and grief and darkness lie,
If but within our bosom's bound
We hold a bright unsullied sky,
Warm with ten thousand mingled rays
Of suns that know no winter days?

Reason indeed may oft complain
For Nature's sad reality,
And tell the suffering heart how vain
Its cherished dreams must always be;
And Truth may rudely trample down
The flowers of Fancy newly blown.

But thou art ever there to bring
The hovering visions back and breathe
New glories o'er the blighted spring
And call a lovelier life from death,
And whisper with a voice divine
Of real worlds as bright as thine.

I trust not to thy phantom bliss,
Yet still in evening's quiet hour
With never-failing thankfulness I
welcome thee, benignant power,
Sure solacer of human cares
And brighter hope when hope despairs.

Death, That Struck When I Was Most Confiding

Death, that struck when I was most confiding
In my certain Faith of joy to be,
Strike again, Time's withered branch dividing
From the fresh root of Eternity!

Leaves, upon Time's branch, were growing brightly,
Full of sap and full of silver dew;
Birds, beneath its shelter, gathered nightly;
Daily, round its flowers, the wild bees flew.

Sorrow passed and plucked the golden blossom,
Guilt stripped off the foliage in its pride;
But, within its parent's kindly bosom,
Flowed forever Life's restoring tide.

Little mourned I for the parted Gladness,
For the vacant nest and silent song;
Hope was there and laughed me out of sadness,
Whispering, "Winter will not linger long."

And behold, with tenfold increase blessing
Spring adorned the beauty-burdened spray;
Wind and rain and fervent heat caressing
Lavished glory on its second May.

High it rose; no winge'd grief could sweep it;
Sin was scared to distance with its shine:
Love and its own life had power to keep it
From all 'Wrong, from every blight but thine!

Heartless' Death, the young leaves droop and languish!
Evening's gentle air may still restore –
No: the morning sunshine mocks my anguish
Time for me must never blossom more!

Strike it down, that other boughs may flourish
Where that perished sapling used to be;
Thus, at least, its mouldering corpse will nourish
That from which it sprung-Eternity.

Part II

Child of Delight! with sun-bright hair
And sea-blue, sea-deep eyes;
Spirit of Bliss, what brings thee here,
Beneath these sullen skies?

Thou shouldest live in eternal spring,
Where endless day is never dim;
Why, seraph, has thy erring wing
Borne thee down to weep with him?

Ah, not from heaven am I descended,
And I do not come to mingle tears;
But sweet is day though with shadows blended;
And, though clouded, sweet are youthful years -

I, the image of light and gladness,
Saw and pitied that mournful boy;
And I swore to take his gloomy sadness,
And give to him my beamy joy -

Heavy and dark the night is closing;
Heavy and dark may its biding be;
Better for all from grief reposing,
And better for all who watch like me –

Guardian angel, he lacks no longer;
Evil fortune he need not fear;
Fate is strong—but Love is stronger,
And more unsleeping than angel's care.

How Beautiful The Earth Is Still

How beautiful the Earth is still
To thee – how full of Happiness;
How little fraught with real ill
Or shadowy phantoms of distress;

How Spring can bring thee glory yet
And Summer win thee to forget
December's sullen time!
Why dost thou hold the treasure fast
Of youth's delight, when youth is past
And thou art near thy prime?

When those who were thy own compeers,
Equal in fortunes and in years,
Have seen their morning melt in tears,
To dull unlovely day;
Blest, had they died unproved and young
Before their hearts were wildly wrung,
Poor slaves, subdued by passions strong,
A weak and helpless prey!

"Because, I hoped while they enjoyed,
And by fulfilment, hope destroyed
As children hope, with trustful breast,
I waited Bliss and cherished Rest.

"A thoughtful Spirit taught me soon
That we must long till life be done;
That every phase of earthly joy
Will always fade and always cloy--

"This I foresaw, and would not chase
The fleeting treacheries,
But with firm foot and tranquil face
Held backward from the tempting race,
Gazed o'er the sands the waves efface
To the enduring seas –

"There cast my anchor of Desire
Deep in unknown Eternity;
Nor ever let my Spirit tire
With looking for What is to be.

"It is Hope's spell that glorifies
Like youth to my maturer eyes
All Nature's million mysteries--
The fearful and the fair–

"Hope soothes me in the griefs I know,
She lulls my pain for others' woe
And makes me strong to undergo
What I am born to bear.
"Glad comforter, will I not brave
Unawed the darkness of the grave?
Nay, smile to hear Death's billows rave,
My Guide, sustained by thee?

The more unjust seems present fate
The more my Spirit springs elate
Strong in thy strength, to anticipate
Rewarding Destiny!

The Prisoner. A Fragment

In the dungeon crypts idly did I stray,
Reckless of the lives wasting there away;
"Draw the ponderous bars; open, Warder stern!"
He dare not say me nay—the hinges harshly turn.

"Our guests are darkly lodged," I whispered, gazing through
The vault whose grated eye showed heaven more grey than blue.
(This was when glad spring laughed in awaking pride.)
"Aye, darkly lodged enough!" returned my sullen guide.

Then, God forgive my youth, forgive my careless tongue!
I scoffed, as the chill chains on the damp flagstones rung;
"Confined in triple walls, art thou so much to fear,
That we must bind thee down and clench thy fetters here?"

The captive raised her face; it was as soft and mild
As sculptured marble saint or slumbering, unweaned child;
It was so soft and mild, it was so sweet and fair,
Pain could not trace a line nor grief a shadow there!

The captive raised her hand and pressed it to her brow:
"I have been struck," she said, "and I am suffering now;
Yet these are little worth, your bolts and irons strong;
And were they forged in steel they could not hold me long."

Hoarse laughed the jailor grim: "Shall I be won to hear;
Dost think, fond dreaming wretch, that I shall grant thy prayer?
Or, better still, wilt melt my master's heart with groans?
Ah, sooner might the sun thaw down these granite stones!

"My master's voice is low, his aspect bland and kind,
But hard as hardest flint the soul that lurks behind;
And I am rough and rude, yet not more rough to see
Than is the hidden ghost which has its home in me!

About her lips there played a smile of almost scorn:
"My friend," she gently said, "you have not heard me mourn;
When you my parents' lives-my lost life, can restore,
Then may I weep and sue-but never, Friend, before!"

"Yet, tell them, Julian, all, I am not doomed to wear
Year after year in gloom and desolate despair;
A messenger of Hope comes every night to me,
And offers, for short life, eternal liberty.

He comes with western winds, with evening's wandering airs,
With that clear dusk of heaven that brings the thickest stars;
Winds take a pensive tone, and stars a tender fire,   And
visions rise and change which kill me with desire—

"Desire for nothing known in my maturer years
When joy grew mad with awe at counting future tears;
When, if my spirit's sky was full of flashes warm,
I knew not whence they came, from sun or thunderstorm;

"But first a hush of peace, a soundless calm descends;
The struggle of distress and fierce impatience ends;
Mute music soothes my breast-unuttered harmony
That I could never dream till earth was lost to me.

"Then dawns the Invisible, the Unseen its truth reveals;
My outward sense is gone, my inward essence feels
Its wings are almost free, its home, its harbour found;
Measuring the gulf it stoops and dares the final bound!

"Oh, dreadful is the check-intense the agony
When the ear begins to hear and the eye begins to see;
When the pulse begins to throb, the brain to think again,
The soul to feel the flesh and the flesh to feel the chain!

"Yet I would lose no sting, would wish no torture less; go
The more that anguish racks the earlier it will bless;
And robed in fires of Hell, or bright with heavenly shine,
If it but herald Death, the vision is divine."

She ceased to speak, and we, unanswering turned to go—
We had no further power to work the captive woe;
Her cheek, he gleaming eye, declared that man had given
A sentence unapproved, and overruled by Heaven.

The Visionary

Silent is the House-all are laid asleep;
One, alone, looks out o'er the snow wreaths deep;
Watching every cloud, dreading every breeze
That whirls the 'wildering drifts and bends the groaning trees.

Cheerful is the hearth, soft the matted floor;
Not one shivering gust creeps through pane or door;
The little lamp burns straight, its rays shoot strong and far;
I trim it well to be the Wanderer's guiding-star.

Frown, my haughty sire; chide, my angry dame;
Set your slaves to spy, threaten me with shame:
But neither sire nor dame, nor prying serf shall know
What angel nightly tracks that waste of winter snow.

What I love shall come like visitant of air,
Safe in secret power from lurking human snare;
Who loves me, no word of mine shall e'er betray,
Though for faith unstained my life must forfeit pay.

Burn, then, little lamp; glimmer straight and clear
Hush! a rustling wing stirs, methinks, the air:
He for whom I wait, thus ever comes to me;
Strange Power! I trust thy might; trust thou my constancy.

No Coward Soul Is Mine

No coward soul is mine
No trembler in the world's storm-troubled sphere
I see Heaven's glories shine
And Faith shines equal arming me from Fear

0 God within my breast
Almighty ever-present Deity
Life, that in me hast rest
As I Undying Life, have power in Thee!

Vain are the thousand creeds
That move men's hearts, unutterably vain,
Worthless as withered weeds
Or idlest froth amid the boundless main

To waken doubt in one
Holding so fast by thy infinity
So surely anchored on
The steadfast rock of Immortality

With wide-embracing love
Thy spirit animates eternal years
Pervades and broods above,
Changes, sustains, dissolves, creates and rears

Though Earth and moon were gone
And suns and universes ceased to be
And thou wert left alone
Every Existence would exist in thee

There is not room for Death
Nor atom that his might could render void
Since thou art Being and Breath
And what thou art may never be destroyed.

Often Rebuked, Yet Always Back Returning

Often rebuked, yet always back returning
To those first feelings that were born with me,
And leaving busy chase of wealth and learning
For idle dreams of things which cannot be:

To-day, I will seek not the shadowy region;
Its unsustaining vastness waxes drear;
And visions rising, legion after legion,
Bring the unreal world too strangely near.

I'll walk, but not in old heroic traces,
And not in paths of high morality,
And not among the half-distinguished faces,
The clouded forms of long-past history.

I'll walk where my own nature would be leading:
It vexes me to choose another guide:
Where the grey flocks in ferny glens are feeding;
Where the wild wind blows on the mountain side

What have those lonely mountains worth revealing?
More glory and more grief than I can tell:
The earth that wakes one human heart to feeling
Can centre both the worlds of Heaven and Hell.

I Am The Only Being Whose Doom

I am the only being whose doom
No tongue would ask no eye would mourn
I never caused a thought of gloom
A smile of joy since I was born

In secret pleasure - secret tears
This changeful life has slipped away
As friendless after eighteen years
As lone as on my natal day

There have been times I cannot hide
There have been times when this was drear
When my sad soul forgot its pride
And longed for one to love me here

But those were in the early glow
Of feelings since subdued by care
And they have died so long ago
I hardly now believe they were

First melted off the hope of youth
Then Fancy's rainbow fast withdrew
And then experience told me truth
In mortal bosoms never grew

'Twas grief enough to think mankind
All hollow servile insincere -
But worse to trust to my own mind
And find the same corruption there

A Little While, A Little While

A little while, a little while,
The weary task is put away,
And I can sing and I can smile,
Alike, while I have holiday.

Why wilt thou go, my harassed heart,
What thought, what scene invites thee now?
What spot, or near or far,
Has rest for thee, my weary brow?

There is a spot, mid barren hills,
Where winter howls, and driving rain;
But if the dreary tempest chills,
There is a light that warms again.

The house is old, the trees are bare,
Moonless above bends twilight's dome;
But what on earth is half so dear,
So longed for, as the hearth of home?

The mute bird sitting on the stone,
The dank moss dripping from the wall,
The thorn-trees gaunt, the walks o'ergrown,
I love them, how I love them all!

Still, as I mused, the naked room,
The alien firelight died away,
And from the midst of cheerless gloom
I passed to bright unclouded day.

A little and a lone green lane
That opened on a common wide;
A distant, dreamy, dim blue chain
Of mountains circling every side;

A heaven so clear, an earth so calm,
So sweet, so soft, so hushed an air;
And, deepening still the dream-like charm,
Wild moor-sheep feeding everywhere.

That was the scene, I knew it well;
I knew the turfy pathway's sweep
That, winding o'er each billowy swell,
Marked out the tracks of wandering sheep.

Could I have lingered but an hour,
It well had paid a week of toil;
But Truth has banished Fancy's power:
Restraint and heavy task recoil.

Even as I stood with raptured eye,
Absorbed in bliss so deep and dear,
My hour of rest had fleeted by,
And back came labour, bondage, care.

Love And Friendship

Love is like the wild rose-briar,

Friendship like the holly-tree --

The holly is dark when the rose-briar blooms

But which will bloom most contantly?

The wild-rose briar is sweet in the spring,

Its summer blossoms scent the air;

Yet wait till winter comes again

And who will call the wild-briar fair?

Then scorn the silly rose-wreath now

And deck thee with the holly's sheen,

That when December blights thy brow

He may still leave thy garland green.

Fall Leaves Fall

Fall, leaves, fall; die, flowers, away;
Lengthen night and shorten day;
Every leaf speaks bliss to me
Fluttering from the autumn tree.

I shall smile when wreaths of snow
Blossom where the rose should grow;
I shall sing when night's decay
Ushers in a drearier day.

My Comforter

Well hast thou spoken, and yet, not taught
A feeling strange or new;
Thou hast but roused a latent thought,
A cloud-closed beam of sunshine, brought
To gleam in open view.

Deep down, concealed within my soul,
That light lies hid from men;
Yet, glows unquenched - though shadows roll,
Its gentle ray cannot control,
About the sullen den.

Was I not vexed, in these gloomy ways
To walk alone so long?
Around me, wretches uttering praise,
Or howling o'er their hopeless days,
And each with Frenzy's tongue; -

A brotherhood of misery,
Their smiles as sad as sighs;
Whose madness daily maddened me,
Distorting into agony
The bliss before my eyes!

So stood I, in Heaven's glorious sun,
And in the glare of Hell;
My spirit drank a mingled tone,
Of seraph's song, and demon's moan;
What my soul bore, my soul alone
Within itself may tell!

Like a soft air, above a sea,
Tossed by the tempest's stir;
A thaw-wind, melting quietly
The snow-drift, on some wintry lea;
No: what sweet thing resembles thee,
My thoughtful Comforter?

And yet a little longer speak,
Calm this resentful mood;
And while the savage heart grows meek,
For other token do not seek,
But let the tear upon my cheek
Evince my gratitude!

A Death – Scene

"O day! he cannot die
When thou so fair art shining!
O Sun, in such a glorious sky,
So tranquilly declining;

He cannot leave thee now,
While fresh west winds are blowing,
And all around his youthful brow
Thy cheerful light is glowing!

Edward, awake, awake -
The golden evening gleams
Warm and bright on Arden's lake -
Arouse thee from thy dreams!

Beside thee, on my knee,
My dearest friend! I pray
That thou, to cross the eternal sea,
Wouldst yet one hour delay:

I hear its billows roar -
I see them foaming high;
But no glimpse of a further shore
Has blest my straining eye.

Believe not what they urge
Of Eden isles beyond;
Turn back, from that tempestuous surge,
To thy own native land.

It is not death, but pain
That struggles in thy breast -
Nay, rally, Edward, rouse again;
I cannot let thee rest!"

One long look, that sore reproved me
For the woe I could not bear -
One mute look of suffering moved me
To repent my useless prayer:

And, with sudden check, the heaving
Of distraction passed away;
Not a sign of further grieving
Stirred my soul that awful day.

Paled, at length, the sweet sun setting;
Sunk to peace the twilight breeze:
Summer dews fell softly, wetting
Glen, and glade, and silent trees.

Then his eyes began to weary,
Weighed beneath a mortal sleep;
And their orbs grew strangely dreary,
Clouded, even as they would weep.

But they wept not, but they changed not,
Never moved, and never closed;
Troubled still, and still they ranged not -
Wandered not, nor yet reposed!

So I knew that he was dying -
Stooped, and raised his languid head;
Felt no breath, and heard no sighing,
So I knew that he was dead.

A Little Budding Rose

It was a little budding rose,
Round like a fairy globe,
And shyly did its leaves unclose
Hid in their mossy robe,
But sweet was the slight and spicy smell
It breathed from its heart invisible.

The rose is blasted, withered, blighted,
Its root has felt a worm,
And like a heart beloved and slighted,
Failed, faded, shrunk its form.

Bud of beauty, bonnie flower,
I stole thee from thy natal bower.

I was the worm that withered thee,
Thy tears of dew all fell for me;
Leaf and stalk and rose are gone,
Exile earth they died upon.

Yes, that last breath of balmy scent
With alien breezes sadly blent!

Anticipation

How beautiful the earth is still,
To thee - how full of happiness!
How little fraught with real ill,
Or unreal phantoms of distress!
How spring can bring thee glory, yet,
And summer win thee to forget
December's sullen time!
Why dost thou hold the treasure fast,
Of youth's delight, when youth is past,
And thou art near thy prime?

When those who were thy own compeers,
Equals in fortune and in years,
Have seen their morning melt in tears,
To clouded, smileless day;
Blest, had they died untried and young,
Before their hearts went wandering wrong,
Poor slaves, subdued by passions strong,
A weak and helpless prey!

"Because, I hoped while they enjoyed,
And, by fulfilment, hope destroyed;
As children hope, with trustful breast,
I waited bliss - and cherished rest.

A thoughtful spirit taught me, soon,
That we must long till life be done;
That every phase of earthly joy
Must always fade, and always cloy:

This I foresaw - and would not chase
The fleeting treacheries;
But, with firm foot and tranquil face,
Held backward from that tempting race,
Gazed o'er the sands the waves efface,
To the enduring seas - ;
There cast my anchor of desire
Deep in unknown eternity;
Nor ever let my spirit tire,
With looking for what is to be!

It is hope's spell that glorifies,
Like youth, to my maturer eyes,
All Nature's million mysteries,
The fearful and the fair -
Hope soothes me in the griefs I know;
She lulls my pain for others' woe,
And makes me strong to undergo
What I am born to bear.

Glad comforter! will I not brave,
Unawed, the darkness of the grave?
Nay, smile to hear Death's billows rave -
Sustained, my guide, by thee?
The more unjust seems present fate,
The more my spirit swells elate,
Strong, in thy strength, to anticipate
Rewarding destiny!"

At Castle Wood

The day is done, the winter sun
Is setting in its sullen sky;
And drear the course that has been run,
And dim the hearts that slowly die.

No star will light my coming night;
No morn of hope for me will shine;
I mourn not heaven would blast my sight,
And I ne'er longed for joys divine.

Through life's hard task I did not ask
Celestial aid, celestial cheer;
I saw my fate without its mask,
And met it too without a tear.

The grief that pressed my aching breast
Was heavier far than earth can be;
And who would dread eternal rest
When labour's hour was agony?

Dark falls the fear of this despair
On spirits born of happiness;
But I was bred the mate of care,
The foster-child of sore distress.

No sighs for me, no sympathy,
No wish to keep my soul below;
The heart is dead in infancy,
Unwept-for let the body go.

The Philosopher

"Enough of thought, philosopher!
Too long hast thou been dreaming
Unlightened, in this chamber drear,
While summer's sun is beaming!
Space - sweeping soul, what sad refrain
Concludes thy musings once again?

"Oh, for the time when I shall sleep
Without identity,
And never care how rain may steep,
Or snow may cover me!
No promised heaven, these wild desires,
Could all, or half fulfil;
No threatened hell, with quenchless fires,
Subdue this quenchless will!"

"So said I, and still say the same;
Still, to my death, will say -
Three gods, within this little frame,
Are warring night and day;
Heaven could not hold them all, and yet
They all are held in me;
And must be mine till I forget
My present entity!
Oh, for the time, when in my breast
Their struggles will be o'er!
Oh, for the day, when I shall rest,
And never suffer more!"

"I saw a spirit, standing, man,
Where thou dost stand - an hour ago,
And round his feet three rivers ran,
Of equal depth, and equal flow -
"A golden stream - and one like blood;
And one like sapphire, seemed to be;
But, where they joined their triple flood
It tumbled in an inky sea.

The spirit sent his dazzling gaze
Down through that ocean's gloomy night
Then, kindling all, with sudden blaze,
The glad deep sparkled wide and bright -
White as the sun, far, far more fair
Than its divided sources were!"

"And even for that spirit, seer,
I've watched and sought my life - time long;
Sought him in heaven, hell, earth and air -
An endless search, and always wrong!
Had I but seen his glorious eye
Once light the clouds that wilder me,
I ne'er had raised this coward cry
To cease to think and cease to be;
I ne'er had called oblivion blest,
Nor, stretching eager hands to death,
Implored to change for senseless rest
This sentient soul, this living breath -
Oh, let me die - that power and will
Their cruel strife may close;
And conquered good, and conquering ill
Be lost in one repose!"

The Sun Has Set

The sun has set, and the long grass now
Waves dreamily in the evening wind;
And the wild bird has flown from that old grey stone
In some warm nook a couch to find.

In all the lonely landscape round
I see no light and hear no sound,
Except the wind that far away
Come sighing o'er the healthy sea.

How Clear She Shines

How clear she shines! How quietly
I lie beneath her guardian light;
While heaven and earth are whispering me,
"Tomorrow, wake, but, dream to-night."

Yes, Fancy, come, my Fairy love!
These throbbing temples softly kiss;
And bend my lonely couch above
And bring me rest, and bring me bliss.

The world is going; dark world, adieu!
Grim world, conceal thee till the day;
The heart, thou canst not all subdue,
Must still resist, if thou delay!

Thy love I will not, will not share;
Thy hatred only wakes a smile;
Thy griefs may wound - thy wrongs may tear,
But, oh, thy lies shall ne'er beguile!
While gazing on the stars that glow
Above me, in that stormless sea,
I long to hope that all the woe
Creation knows, is held in thee!

And, this shall be my dream to-night;
I'll think the heaven of glorious spheres
Is rolling on its course of light
In endless bliss, through endless years;
I'll think, there's not one world above,
Far as these straining eyes can see,
Where Wisdom ever laughed at Love,
Or Virtue crouched to Infamy;

Where, writhing 'neath the strokes of Fate,
The mangled wretch was forced to smile;
To match his patience 'gainst her hate,
His heart rebellious all the while.

Where Pleasure still will lead to wrong,
And helpless Reason warn in vain;
And Truth is weak, and Treachery strong;
And Joy the surest path to Pain;
And Peace, the lethargy of Grief;
And Hope, a phantom of the soul;
And Life, a labour, void and brief;
And Death, the despot of the whole!

Honours Martyr

The moon is full this winter night;
The stars are clear, though few;
And every window glistens bright,
With leaves of frozen dew.

The sweet moon through your lattice gleams
And lights your room like day;
And there you pass, in happy dreams,
The peaceful hours away!

While I, with effort hardly quelling
The anguish in my breast,
Wander about the silent dwelling,
And cannot think of rest.

The old clock in the gloomy hall
Ticks on, from hour to hour;
And every time its measured call
Seems lingering slow and slower:

And oh, how slow that keen-eyed star
Has tracked the chilly grey!
What, watching yet! how very far
The morning lies away!

Without your chamber door I stand;
Love, are you slumbering still?
My cold heart, underneath my hand,
Has almost ceased to thrill.

Bleak, bleak the east wind sobs and sighs,
And drowns the turret bell,
Whose sad note, undistinguished, dies
Unheard, like my farewell!

To-morrow, Scorn will blight my name,
And Hate will trample me,
Will load me with a coward's shame?
A traitor's perjury.

False friends will launch their covert sneers;
True friends will wish me dead;
And I shall cause the bitterest tears
That you have ever shed.

The dark deeds of my outlawed race
Will then like virtues shine;
And men will pardon their disgrace,
Beside the guilt of mine.

For, who forgives the accursed crime
Of dastard treachery?
Rebellion, in its chosen time,
May Freedom's champion be;

Revenge may stain a righteous sword,
It may be just to slay;
But, traitor, traitor, from that word
All true breasts shrink away!

Oh, I would give my heart to death,
To keep my honour fair;
Yet, I'll not give my inward faith
My honour's name to spare!

Not even to keep your priceless love,
Dare I, Beloved, deceive;
This treason should the future prove,
Then, only then, believe!

I know the path I ought to go;
I follow fearlessly,
Inquiring not what deeper woe
Stern duty stores for me.

So foes pursue, and cold allies
Mistrust me, every one:
Let me be false in others' eyes,
If faithful in my own.

Self-Interrogation

The evening passes fast away,
'Tis almost time to rest;
What thoughts has left the vanished day,
What feelings, in thy breast?

"The vanished day? It leaves a sense
Of labour hardly done;
Of little, gained with vast expense, -
A sense of grief alone!

"Time stands before the door of Death,
Upbraiding bitterly;
And Conscience, with exhaustless breath,
Pours black reproach on me:

"And though I've said that Conscience lies,
And Time should Fate condemn;
Still, sad Repentance clouds my eyes,
And makes me yield to them!

"Then art thou glad to seek repose?
Art glad to leave the sea,
And anchor all thy weary woes
In calm Eternity?

"Nothing regrets to see thee go -
Not one voice sobs "farewell,"
And where thy heart has suffered so,
Canst thou desire to dwell?"

"Alas! The countless links are strong
That bind us to our clay;
The loving spirit lingers long,
And would not pass away!

"And rest is sweet, when laurelled fame
Will crown the soldier's crest;
But, a brave heart, with a tarnished name,
Would rather fight than rest."

"Well, thou hast fought for many a year,
Hast fought thy whole life through,
Hast humbled Falsehood, trampled Fear;
What is there left to do?"

"'Tis true, this arm has hotly striven,
Has dared what few would dare;
Much have I done, and freely given,
But little learnt to bear!"

"Look on the grave, where thou must sleep,
Thy last, and strongest foe;
It is endurance not to weep,
If that repose seem woe.

"The long war closing in defeat,
Defeat serenely borne,
Thy midnight rest may still be sweet,
And break in glorious morn!"

How Still, How Happy!

How still, how happy! Those are words
That once would scarce agree together;
I loved the plashing of the surge -
The changing heaven the breezy weather,

More than smooth seas and cloudless skies
And solemn, soothing, softened airs
That in the forest woke no sighs
And from the green spray shook no tears.

How still, how happy! now I feel
Where silence dwells is sweeter far
Than laughing mirth's most joyous swell
However pure its raptures are.

Come, sit down on this sunny stone:
'Tis wintry light o'er flowerless moors -
But sit - for we are all alone
And clear expand heaven's breathless shores.

I could think in the withered grass
Spring's budding wreaths we might discern;
The violet's eye might shyly flash
And young leaves shoot among the fern.

It is but thought - full many a night
The snow shall clothe those hills afar
And storms shall add a drearier blight
And winds shall wage a wilder war,

Before the lark may herald in
Fresh foliage twined with blossoms fair
And summer days again begin
Their glory - haloed crown to wear.

Yet my heart loves December's smile
As much as July's golden beam;
Then let us sit and watch the while
The blue ice curdling on the stream -

The Blue Bell

The blue bell is the sweetest flower
That waves in summer air;
Its blossoms have the mightiest power
To soothe my spirit's care.

There is a spell in purple heath
Too wildly, sadly dear;
The violet has a fragrant breath
But fragrance will not cheer.

The trees are bare, the sun is cold;
And seldom, seldom seen;
The heavens have lost their zone of gold
The earth its robe of green;

And ice upon the glancing stream
Has cast its sombre shade
And distant hills and valleys seem
In frozen mist arrayed -

The blue bell cannot charm me now
The heath has lost its bloom,
The violets in the glen below
They yield no sweet perfume.

But though I mourn the heather-bell
'Tis better far, away;
I know how fast my tears would swell
To see it smile today;

And that wood flower that hides so shy
Beneath the mossy stone
Its balmy scent and dewy eye:
'Tis not for them I moan.

It is the slight and stately stem,
The blossom's silvery blue,
The buds hid like a sapphire gem
In sheaths of emerald hue.

'Tis these that breathe upon my heart
A calm and softening spell
That if it makes the tear-drop start
Has power to soothe as well.

For these I weep, so long divided
Through winter's dreary day,
In longing weep--but most when guided
On withered banks to stray.

If chilly then the light should fall
Adown the dreary sky
And gild the dank and darkened wall
With transient brilliancy,

How do I yearn, how do I pine
For the time of flowers to come,
And turn me from that fading shine
To mourn the fields of home -

Come Hither, Child

Come hither, child--who gifted thee
With power to touch that string so well?
How darest thou rouse up thoughts in me,
Thoughts that I would--but cannot quell?

Nay, chide not, lady; long ago
I heard those notes in Ula's hall,
And had I known they'd waken woe
I'd weep their music to recall.

But thus it was: one festal night
When I was hardly six years old
I stole away from crowds and light
And sought a chamber dark and cold.

I had no one to love me there,
I knew no comrade and no friend;
And so I went to sorrow where
Heaven, only heaven saw me bend.

Loud blew the wind; 'twas sad to stay
From all that splendour barred away.

I imaged in the lonely room
A thousand forms of fearful gloom.

And with my wet eyes raised on high
I prayed to God that I might die.

Suddenly in that silence drear
A sound of music reached my ear,

And then a note, I hear it yet,
So full of soul, so deeply sweet,
I thought that Gabriel's self had come
To take me to thy father's home.

Three times it rose, that seraph strain,
Then died, nor breathed again;
But still the words and still the tone
Dwell round my heart when all alone.

Death!

Death! that struck when I was most confiding
In my certain faith of joy to be -
Strike again, Time's withered branch dividing
From the fresh root of Eternity!

Leaves, upon Time's branch, were growing brightly,
Full of sap, and full of silver dew;
Birds beneath its shelter gathered nightly;
Daily round its flowers the wild bees flew.

Sorrow passed, and plucked the golden blossom;
Guilt stripped off the foliage in its pride;
But, within its parent's kindly bosom,
Flowed for ever Life's restoring-tide.

Little mourned I for the parted gladness,
For the vacant nest and silent song -
Hope was there, and laughed me out of sadness;
Whispering, " Winter will not linger long!"

And, behold! with tenfold increase blessing,
Spring adorned the beauty-burdened spray;
Wind and rain and fervent heat, caressing,
Lavished glory on that second May!

High it rose - no winged grief could sweep it;
Sin was scared to distance with its shine;
Love, and its own life, had power to keep it
From all wrong - from every blight but thine!

Cruel Death! The young leaves droop and languish;
Evening's gentle air may still restore -
No! the morning sunshine mocks my anguish -
Time, for me, must never blossom more!

Strike it down, that other boughs may flourish
Where that perished sapling used to be;
Thus, at least, its mouldering corpse will nourish
That from which it sprung - Eternity.

Faith And Despondency

The winter wind is loud and wild,
Come close to me, my darling child;
Forsake thy books, and mateless play;
And, while the night is gathering grey,
We'll talk its pensive hours away;--

'Ierne, round our sheltered hall
November's gusts unheeded call;
Not one faint breath can enter here
Enough to wave my daughter's hair,
And I am glad to watch the blaze
Glance from her eyes, with mimic rays;
To feel her cheek so softly pressed,
In happy quiet on my breast.

'But, yet, even this tranquillity
Brings bitter, restless thoughts to me;
And, in the red fire's cheerful glow,
I think of deep glens, blocked with snow;
I dream of moor, and misty hill,
Where evening closes dark and chill;
For, lone, among the mountains cold,
Lie those that I have loved of old.

And my heart aches, in hopeless pain
Exhausted with repinings vain,
That I shall greet them ne'er again!'

'Father, in early infancy,
When you were far beyond the sea,
Such thoughts were tyrants over me!
I often sat, for hours together,
Through the long nights of angry weather,
Raised on my pillow, to descry
The dim moon struggling in the sky;

Or, with strained ear, to catch the shock,
Of rock with wave, and wave with rock;
So would I fearful vigil keep,
And, all for listening, never sleep.
But this world's life has much to dread,
Not so, my Father, with the dead.

'Oh! not for them, should we despair,
The grave is drear, but they are not there;
Their dust is mingled with the sod,
Their happy souls are gone to God!
You told me this, and yet you sigh,
And murmur that your friends must die.
Ah! my dear father, tell me why?

For, if your former words were true,
How useless would such sorrow be;
As wise, to mourn the seed which grew
Unnoticed on its parent tree,
Because it fell in fertile earth,
And sprang up to a glorious birth--
Struck deep its root, and lifted high
Its green boughs, in the breezy sky.

'But, I'll not fear, I will not weep
For those whose bodies rest in sleep,--
I know there is a blessed shore,
Opening its ports for me, and mine;
And, gazing Time's wide waters o'er,
I weary for that land divine,
Where we were born, where you and I
Shall meet our Dearest, when we die;
From suffering and corruption free,
Restored into the Deity.'

'Well hast thou spoken, sweet, trustful child!
And wiser than thy sire;
And worldly tempests, raging wild,
Shall strengthen thy desire--
Thy fervent hope, through storm and foam,
Through wind and ocean's roar,
To reach, at last, the eternal home,
The steadfast, changeless, shore!'

Far Away Is Mirth Withdrawn

Far, far away is mirth withdrawn
'Tis three long hours before the morn
And I watch lonely, drearily -
So come thou shade commune with me

Deserted one ! thy corpse lies cold
And mingled with a foreign mould -
Year after year the grass grows green
Above the dust where thou hast been.

I will not name thy blighted name
Tarnished by unforgotten shame
Though not because my bosom torn
Joins the mad world in all its scorn -

Thy phantom face is dark with woe
Tears have left ghastly traces there,
Those ceaseless tears ! I wish their flow
Could quench thy wild despair.

They deluge my heart like the rain
On cursed Gomorrah's howling plain -
Yet when I hear thy foes deride
I must cling closely to thy side -

Our mutual foes - they will not rest
From trampling on thy buried breast -
Glutting there hatred with the doom
They picture thine, beyond the tomb -

But God is not like human kind
Man cannot read the Almighty mind
Vengeance will never torture they
Nor hunt thy soul eternally

Then do not in this night of grief
This time of over whelming fear
O do not think that God can leave
Forget, forsake, refuse to hear ! -

What have I dreamt ? He lies asleep
With whom my heart would vainly weep
He rests - and I endure the woe
That left his spirit long ago -

Hope

Hope was but a timid friend;
She sat without the grated den,
Watching how my fate would tend,
Even as selfish-hearted men.

She was cruel in her fear;
Through the bars, one dreary day,
I looked out to see her there,
And she turned her face away!

Like a false guard, false watch keeping,
Still, in strife, she whispered peace;
She would sing while I was weeping;
If I listened, she would cease.

False she was, and unrelenting;
When my last joys strewed the ground,
Even Sorrow saw, repenting,
Those sad relics scattered round;

Hope, whose whisper would have given
Balm to all my frenzied pain,
Stretched her wings, and soared to heaven,
Went, and ne'er returned again!

I See Around Me Tombstones Grey

I see around me tombstones grey
Stretching their shadows far away.
Beneath the turf my footsteps tread
Lie low and lone the silent dead -
Beneath the turf - beneath the mould -
Forever dark, forever cold -
And my eyes cannot hold the tears
That memory hoards from vanished years
For Time and Death and Mortal pain
Give wounds that will not heal again -
Let me remember half the woe
I've seen and heard and felt below,
And Heaven itself - so pure and blest,
Could never give my spirit rest -
Sweet land of light! thy children fair
Know nought akin to our despair -
Nor have they felt, nor can they tell
What tenants haunt each mortal cell,
What gloomy guests we hold within -
Torments and madness, tears and sin!
Well - may they live in ectasy
Their long eternity of joy;
At least we would not bring them down
With us to weep, with us to groan,
No - Earth would wish no other sphere

To taste her cup of sufferings drear;
She turns from Heaven with a careless eye
And only mourns that we must die!
Ah mother, what shall comfort thee
In all this boundless misery?
To cheer our eager eyes a while
We see thee smile; how fondly smile!
But who reads not through that tender glow
Thy deep, unutterable woe:
Indeed no dazzling land above
Can cheat thee of thy children's love.

We all, in life's departing shine,
Our last dear longings blend with thine;
And struggle still and strive to trace
With clouded gaze, thy darling face.

We would not leave our native home
For any world beyond the Tomb.

No - rather on thy kindly breast
Let us be laid in lasting rest;
Or waken but to share with thee
A mutual immortality -

If Grief For Grief Can Touch Three

If grief for grief can touch thee,
If answering woe for woe,
If any truth can melt thee
Come to me now!

I cannot be more lonely,
More drear I cannot be!
My worn heart beats so wildly
'Twill break for thee--

And when the world despises--
When Heaven repels my prayer--
Will not mine angel comfort?
Mine idol hear?

Yes, by the tears I'm poured,
By all my hours of pain
O I shall surely win thee,
Beloved, again!

Last Lines

No coward soul is mine,
No trembler in the world's storm-troubled sphere:
I see Heaven's glories shine,
And faith shines equal, arming me from fear.

O God within my breast,
Almighty, ever-present Deity!
Life--that in me has rest,
As I--undying Life--have power in Thee!

Vain are the thousand creeds
That move men's hearts: unutterably vain;
Worthless as wither'd weeds,
Or idlest froth amid the boundless main,

To waken doubt in one
Holding so fast by Thine infinity;
So surely anchor'd on
The steadfast rock of immortality.

With wide-embracing love
Thy Spirit animates eternal years,
Pervades and broods above,
Changes, sustains, dissolves, creates, and rears.

Though earth and man were gone,
And suns and universes cease to be,
And Thou were left alone,
Every existence would exist in Thee.

There is not room for Death,
Nor atom that his might could render void:
Thou--Thou art Being and Breath,
And what Thou art may never be destroyed.

Me Thinks This Heart

Me thinks this heart should rest awhile
So stilly round the evening falls
The veiled sun sheds no parting smile
Nor mirth nor music wakes my Halls

I have sat lonely all the day
Watching the drizzly mist descend
And first conceal the hills in grey
And then along the valleys wend

And I have sat and watched the trees
And the sad flowers how drear they blow
Those flowers were formed to feel the breeze
Wave their light leaves in summer's glow

Yet their lives passed in gloomy woe
And hopeless comes its dark decline
And I lament because I know
That cold departure pictures mine

Mild The Mist Upon The Hill

Mild the mist upon the hill
Telling not of storms tomorrow;
No, the day has wept its fill,
Spent its store of silent sorrow.

O, I'm gone back to the days of youth,
I am a child once more,
And 'neath my father's sheltering roof
And near the old hall door

I watch this cloudy evening fall
After a day of rain;
Blue mists, sweet mists of summer pall
The horizon's mountain chain.

The damp stands on the long green grass
As thick as morning's tears,
And dreamy scents of fragrance pass
That breathe of other years.

Moonlight Summer Moonlight

'Tis moonlight, summer moonlight,
All soft and still and fair;
The solemn hour of midnight
Breathes sweet thoughts everywhere,

But most where trees are sending
Their breezy boughs on high,
Or stooping low are lending
A shelter from the sky.

And there in those wild bowers
A lovely form is laid;
Green grass and dew-steeped flowers
Wave gently round her head.

My Ladys Grave

The linnet in the rocky dells,
The moor-lark in the air,
The bee among the heather bells
That hide my lady fair:

The wild deer browse above her breast;
The wild birds raise their brood;
And they, her smiles of love caress'd,
Have left her solitude!

I ween that when the grave's dark wall
Did first her form retain,
They thought their hearts could ne'er recall
The light of joy again.

They thought the tide of grief would flow
Uncheck'd through future years;
But where is all their anguish now,
And where are all their tears?

Well, let them fight for honour's breath,
Or pleasure's shade pursue--
The dweller in the land of death
Is changed and careless too.

And if their eyes should watch and weep
Till sorrow's source were dry,
She would not, in her tranquil sleep,
Return a single sigh!

Blow, west wind, by the lonely mound:
And murmur, summer streams!
There is no need of other sound
To soothe my lady's dreams.

Night Is Darkening Around Me

The night is darkening round me,
The wild winds coldly blow;
But a tyrant spell has bound me,
And I cannot, cannot go.

The giant trees are bending
Their bare boughs weighed with snow;
The storm is fast descending,
And yet I cannot go.

Clouds beyond clouds above me,
Wastes beyond wastes below;
But nothing drear can move me:
I will not, cannot go

Oh For The Time When I Shall Sleep

Oh, for the time when I shall sleep
Without identity,
And never care how rain may steep,
Or snow may cover me!
No promised heaven these wild desires
Could all, or half, fulfil;
No threatened hell, with quenchless fires,
Subdue this quenchless will!

So said I, and still say the same;
Still, to my death, will say—
Three gods within this little frame
Are warring night and day:
Heaven could not hold them all, and yet
They all are held in me;
And must be mine till I forget
My present entity!

Oh, for the time when in my breast
Their struggles will be o'er!
Oh, for the day when I shall rest,
And never suffer more!

Plead For Me

Oh, thy bright eyes must answer now,
When Reason, with a scornful brow,
Is mocking at my overthrow!
Oh, thy sweet tongue must plead for me
And tell, why I have chosen thee!

Stern Reason is to judgment come,
Arrayed in all her forms of gloom:
Wilt thou, my advocate, be dumb?
No, radiant angel, speak and say,
Why I did cast the world away.

Why I have persevered to shun
The common paths that others run,
And on a strange road journeyed on,
Heedless, alike, of wealth and power -
Of glory's wreath and pleasure's flower.

These, once, indeed, seemed Beings Divine;
And they, perchance, heard vows of mine,
And saw my offerings on their shrine;
But, careless gifts are seldom prized,
And mine were worthily despised.

So, with a ready heart I swore
To seek their altar-stone no more;
And gave my spirit to adore
Thee, ever - present, phantom thing;
My slave, my comrade, and my king,

A slave, because I rule thee still;
Incline thee to my changeful will,
And make thy influence good or ill:
A comrade, for by day and night
Thou art my intimate delight, -

My darling pain that wounds and sears
And wrings a blessing out from tears
By deadening me to earthly cares;
And yet, a king, though Prudence well
Have taught thy subject to rebel.

And am I wrong to worship, where
Faith cannot doubt, nor hope despair,
Since my own soul can grant my prayer?
Speak, God of visions, plead for me,
And tell why I have chosen thee!

Remembrance

Cold in the earth—and the deep snow piled above thee,
Far, far removed, cold in the dreary grave!
Have I forgot, my only Love, to love thee,
Severed at last by Time's all-severing wave?

Now, when alone, do my thoughts no longer hover
Over the mountains, on that northern shore,
Resting their wings where heath and fern-leaves cover
That noble heart for ever, ever more?

Cold in the earth, and fifteen wild Decembers
From those brown hills have melted into spring:
Faithful indeed is the spirit that remembers
After such years of change and suffering!

Sweet Love of youth, forgive if I forget thee,
While the world's tide is bearing me along:
Sterner desires and other hopes beset me,
Hopes which obscure, but cannot do thee wrong!

No later light has lightened up my heaven;
No second morn has ever shone for me:
All my life's bliss from thy dear life was given,
All my life's bliss is in the grave with thee.

But when the days of golden dreams had perished,
And even Despair was powerless to destroy,
Then did I learn how existence could be cherished,
Strengthened, and fed without the aid of joy;

Then did I check the tears of useless passion,
Weaned my young soul from yearning after thine;
Sternly denied its burning wish to hasten
Down to that tomb already more than mine.

And even yet I dare not let it languish,
Dare not indulge in Memory's rapturous pain;
Once drinking deep of that divinest anguish,
How could I seek the empty world again?

Shall Earth No More Inspire Thee

Shall Earth no more inspire thee,
Thou lonely dreamer now?
Since passion may not fire thee
Shall nature cease to bow?

Thy mind is ever moving
In regions dark to thee;
Recall its useless roving -
Come back and dwell with me -

I know my mountain breezes
Enchant and soothe thee still -
I know my sunshine pleases
Despite thy wayward will -

When day with evening blending
Sinks from the summer sky,
I've seen thy spirit bending
In fond idolotry -

I've watched thee every hour -
I know my mighty sway -
I know my magic power
To drive thy griefs away -

Few hearts to mortal given
On earth so wildly pine
Yet none would ask a Heaven
More like this Earth than thine -

Then let my winds caress thee -
Thy comrade let me be -
Since nought beside can bless thee
Return and dwell with me -

She Dried Her Tears

She dried her tears and they did smile
To see her cheeks' returning glow
How little dreaming all the while
That full heart throbbed to overflow

With that sweet look and lively tone
And bright eye shining all the day
They could not guess at midnight lone
How she would weep the time away

Song

The linnet in the rocky dells,
The moor - lark in the air,
The bee among the heather - bells
That hide my lady fair:

The wild deer browse above her breast;
The wild birds raise their brood;
And they, her smiles of love caressed,
Have left their solitude!

I ween, that when the grave's dark wall
Did first her form retain,
They thought their hearts could ne'er recall
The light of joy again.

They thought the tide of grief would flow
Unchecked through future years,
But where is all their anguish now,
And where are all their tears?

Well, let them fight for Honour's breath,
Or Pleasure's shade pursue -
The Dweller in the land of Death
Is changed and careless too.

And if their eyes should watch and weep
Till sorrow's source were dry
She would not, in her tranquil sleep,
Return a single sigh!

Blow, west wind, by the lonely mound,
And murmur, summer streams -
There is no need of other sound
To soothe my Lady's dreams.

Speak God Of Visions

O, thy bright eyes must answer now,
When Reason, with a scornful brow,
Is mocking at my overthrow!
O, thy sweet tongue must plead for me,
And tell why I have chosen thee!

Stern Reason is to judgment come,
Arrayed in all her forms of gloom:
Wilt thou, my advocate, be dumb?
No, radiant angel, speak and say
Why I did cast the world away;

Why I have persevered to shun
The common paths that others run,
And on a strange road journeyed on,
Heedless alike of wealth and power,
Of Glory's wreath and Pleasure's flower.

These once, indeed, seemed Beings Divine;
And they, perchance, heard vows of mine,
And saw my offerings on their shrine;
But careless gifts are seldom prized,
And mine were worthily despised.

So, with a ready heart I swore
To seek their altar-stone no more;
And gave my spirit to adore
Thee, ever-present, phantom thing—
My slave, my comrade, and my king.

A slave, because I rule thee still,
Incline thee to my changeful will,
And make thy influence good or ill;
A comrade, for by day and night
Thou art my intimate delight,—

My darling pain that wounds and sears,
And wrings a blessing out of tears
Be deadening me to earthly cares;
And yet, a king, though Prudence well
Have taught thy subject to rebel.

And I am wrong to worship where
Faith cannot doubt, nor Hope despair,
Since my own soul can grant my prayer?
Speak, God of Visions, plead for me,
And tell why I have chosen thee!

Stanza

Often rebuked, yet always back returning
To those first feelings that were born with me,
And leaving busy chase of wealth and learning
For idle dreams of things which cannot be:

Today, I will seek not the shadowy region;
Its unsustaining vastness waxes drear;
And visions rising, legion after legion,
Bring the unreal world too strangely near.

I'll walk, but not in old heroic traces,
And not in paths of high morality,
And not among the half-distinguished faces,
The clouded forms of long-past history.

I'll walk where my own nature would be leading:
It vexes me to choose another guide:
Where the grey flocks in ferny glens are feeding;
Where the wild wind blows on the mountain side.

What have those lonely mountains worth revealing?
More glory and more grief than I can tell:
The earth that wakes one human heart to feeling
Can centre both the worlds of heaven and hell.

Stanzas

I'll not weep that thou art going to leave me,
There's nothing lovely here;
And doubly will the dark world grieve me,
While thy heart suffers there.

I'll not weep, because the summer's glory
Must always end in gloom;
And, follow out the happiest story -
It closes with a tomb!

And I am weary of the anguish
Increasing winters bear;
Weary to watch the spirit languish
Through years of dead despair.

So, if a tear, when thou art dying,
Should haply fall from me,
It is but that my soul is sighing,
To go and rest with thee.

Stars

Ah! why, because the dazzling sun
Restored our Earth to joy,
Have you departed, every one,
And left a desert sky?

All through the night, your glorious eyes
Were gazing down in mine,
And, with a full heart's thankful sighs,
I blessed that watch divine.

I was at peace, and drank your beams
As they were life to me;
And revelled in my changeful dreams,
Like petrel on the sea.

Thought followed thought, star followed star
Through boundless regions on;
While one sweet influence, near and far,
Thrilled through, and proved us one!

Why did the morning dawn to break
So great, so pure a spell;
And scorch with fire the tranquil cheek,
Where your cool radiance fell?

Blood-red, he rose, and arrow-straight,
His fierce beams struck my brow;
The soul of nature sprang, elate,
But mine sank sad and low.

My lids closed down, yet through their veil
I saw him, blazing, still,
And steep in gold the misty dale,
And flash upon the hill.

I turned me to the pillow, then,
To call back night, and see
Your words of solemn light, again,
Throb with my heart, and me!]

It would not do - the pillow glowed,
And glowed both roof and floor;
And birds sang loudly in the wood,
And fresh winds shook the door;

The curtains waved, the wakened flies
Were murmuring round my room,
Imprisoned there, till I should rise,
And give them leave to roam.

O stars, and dreams, and gentle night;
O night and stars, return!
And hide me from the hostile light
That does not warm, but burn;

That drains the blood of suffering men;
Drinks tears, instead of dew;
Let me sleep through his blinding reign,
And only wake with you!

Sympathy

There should be no despair for you
While nightly stars are burning,
While evening pours its silent dew
And sunshine gilds the morning.

There should be no despair - though tears
May flow down like a river:
Are not the best beloved of years
Around your heart forever?

They weep - you weep - it must be so;
Winds sigh as you are sighing,
And Winter sheds his grief in snow
Where Autumn's leaves are lying:

Yet these revive, and from their fate
Your fate cannot be parted,
Then journey on, if not elate,
Still, never broken-hearted!

That Wind I Used To Hear It Swelling

That wind I used to hear it swelling
With joy divinely deep
You might have seen my hot tears welling
But rapture made me weep

I used to love on winter nights
To lie and dream alone
Of all the hopes and real delights
My early years had known

And oh above the rest of those
That coming time should [bear]
Like heaven's own glorious stars they rose
Still beaming bright and fair

The Night – Wind

In summer's mellow midnight,
A cloudless moon shone through
Our open parlour window,
And rose-trees wet with dew.

I sat in silent musing;
The soft wind waved my hair;
It told me heaven was glorious,
And sleeping earth was fair.

I needed not its breathing
To bring such thoughts to me;
But still it whispered lowly,
'How dark the woods would be!

'The thick leaves in my murmur
Are rustling like a dream,
And all their myriad voices
Instinct with spirit seem.'

I said, 'Go, gentle singer,
Thy wooing voice is kind:
But do not think its music
Has power to reach my mind.

'Play with the scented flower,
The young tree's supply bough,
And leave my human feelings
In their own course to flow.'

The wanderer would not heed me:
Its kiss grew warmer still:
'Oh Come!' it sighed so sweetly;
'I'll win thee 'gainst thy will.

'Were we not friends from childhood?
Have I not loved thee long?
As long as thou, the solemn night,
Whose silence wakes my song.

'And when thy heart is resting
Beneath the church-aisle stone,
I shall have time for mourning,
And thou for being alone.'

The Old Stoic

Riches I hold in light esteem,
And love I laugh to scorn;
And lust of fame was but a dream
That vanish'd with the morn:

And if I pray, the only prayer
That moves my lips for me
Is, "Leave the heart that now I bear,
And give me liberty!"

Yes, as my swift days near their goal,
'Tis all that I implore:
In life and death a chainless soul,
With courage to endure

The Prisoner

Still let my tyrants know, I am not doomed to wear
Year after year in gloom and desolate despair;
A messenger of Hope comes every night to me,
And offers for short life, eternal liberty.

He comes with western winds, with evening's wandering airs,
With that clear dusk of heaven that brings the thickest stars:
Winds take a pensive tone, and stars a tender fire,
And visions rise, and change, that kill me with desire.

Desire for nothing known in my maturer years,
When Joy grew mad with awe, at counting future tears:
When, if my spirit's sky was full of flashes warm,
I knew not whence they came, from sun or thunderstorm.

But first, a hush of peace—a soundless calm descends;
The struggle of distress and fierce impatience ends;
Mute music soothes my breast—unuttered harmony
That I could never dream, till Earth was lost to me.

Then dawns the Invisible; the Unseen its truth reveals;
My outward sense is gone, my inward essence feels;
Its wings are almost free—its home, its harbour found;
Measuring the gulf, it stoops, and dares the final bound.

O dreadful is the check—intense the agony—
When the ear begins to hear, and the eye begins to see;
When the pulse begins to throb, the brain to think again,
The soul to feel the flesh, and the flesh to feel the chain.

Yet I would lose no sting, would wish no torture less;
The more that anguish racks, the earlier it will bless;
And robed in fires of hell, or bright with heavenly shine,
If it but herald Death, the vision is divine.

Wind Was Rough Which Tore

The wind was rough which tore
That leaf from its parent tree
The fate was cruel which bore
The withering corpse to me

We wander on we have no rest
It is a dreary way

What shadow is it
That ever moves before [my] eyes
It has a brow of ghostly whiteness

Yes, Holy Be Thy Resting Place

Yes, holy be thy resting place
Wherever thou may'st lie;
The sweetest winds breathe on thy face,
The softest of the sky.

And will not guardian Angles send
Kind dreams and thoughts of love,
Though I no more may watchful bend
Thy longed repose above?

And will not heaven itself bestow
A beam of glory there
That summer's grass more green may grow,
And summer's flowers more fair?

Farewell, farewell, 'tis hard to part
Yet, loved one, it must be:
I would not rend another heart
Not even by blessing thee.

Go! We must break affection's chain,
Forget the hopes of years:
Nay, grieve not - willest thou remain
To waken wilder tears

This herald breeze with thee and me,
Roved in the dawning day:
And thou shouldest be where it shall be
Ere evening, far away.

Oh, Thy Bright Eyes Must Answer Now

Oh, thy bright eyes must answer now,
When Reason, with a scornful brow,
Is mocking at my overthrow!
Oh, thy sweet tongue must plead for me
And tell why I have chosen thee!.

Stern Reason is to judgment come,
Arrayed in all her forms of gloom:
Wilt thou, my advocate, be dumb?
No, radiant angel, speak and say
Why I did cast the world away,

Why I have persevered to shun
The common paths that others run;
And on a strange road journeyed on,
Heedless, alike of wealth and power
Of glory's wreath and pleasure's flower.

These, once, indeed, seemed Beings Divine;
And they, perchance, heard vows of mine,
And saw my offerings on their shrine;
But careless gifts are seldom prized,
And mine were worthily despised.

So, with a ready heart, I swore
To seek their altar-stone no more;
And gave my spirit to adore
Thee, ever-present, phantom thing
My slave, my comrade, and my king.

A slave, because I rule thee still;
Incline thee to my changeful will,
And make thy influence good or ill:
A comrade, for by day and night
Thou art my intimate delight,

My darling pain that wounds and sears,
And wrings a blessing out from tears
By deadening me to earthly cares;
And yet, a king, though Prudence well
Have taught thy subject to rebel.

And am I wrong to worship where
Faith cannot doubt, nor hope despair,
Since my own soul can grant my prayer?
Speak, God of visions, plead for me,
And tell why I have chosen thee!.

Warning And Reply

In the earth—the earth—thou shalt be laid,
A grey stone standing over thee;
Black mould beneath thee spread,
And black mould to cover thee.

'Well—there is rest there,
So fast come thy prophecy;
The time when my sunny hair
Shall with grass roots entwined be.'

But cold—cold is that resting-place,
Shut out from joy and liberty,
And all who loved thy living face
Will shrink from it shudderingly,

'Not so. Here the world is chill,
And sworn friends fall from me:
But there—they will own me still,
And prize my memory.'

Farewell, then, all that love,
All that deep sympathy:
Sleep on: Heaven laughs above,
Earth never misses thee.

Turf-sod and tombstone drear
Part human company;
One heart breaks only—here,
But that heart was worthy thee!

Loud Without The Wind Was Roaring

Loud without the wind was roaring
Through th' autumnal sky;
Drenching wet, the cold rain pouring,
Spoke of winter nigh.
All too like that dreary eve,
Did my exiled spirit grieve.

Grieved at first, but grieved not long,
Sweet—how softly sweet!—it came;
Wild words of an ancient song,
Undefined, without a name.

'It was spring, and the skylark was singing';
Those words they awakened a spell;
They unlocked a deep fountain, whose springing,
Nor absence, nor distance can quell.

In the gloom of a cloudy November
They uttered the music of May;
They kindled the perishing ember
Into fervour that could not decay.

Awaken, o'er all my dear moorland,
West-wind, in thy glory and pride!
Oh! call me from valley and lowland,
To walk by the hill-torrent's side!

It is swelled with the first snowy weather;
The rocks they are icy and hoar,
And sullenly waves the long heather,
And the fern leaves are sunny no more.

There are no yellow stars on the mountain
The bluebells have long died away
From the brink of the moss-bedded fountain —
From the side of the wintry brae.

But lovelier than corn-fields all waving
In emerald, and vermeil, and gold,
Are the heights where the north-wind is raving,
And the crags where I wandered of old.

It was morning: the bright sun was beaming;
How sweetly it brought back to me
The time when nor labour nor dreaming
Broke the sleep of the happy and free!

But blithely we rose as the dawn-heaven
Was melting to amber and blue,
And swift were the wings to our feet given,
As we traversed the meadows of dew.

For the moors! For the moors, where the short grass
Like velvet beneath us should lie!
For the moors! For the moors, where each high pass
Rose sunny against the clear sky!

For the moors, where the linnet was trilling
Its song on the old granite stone;
Where the lark, the wild sky-lark, was filling
Every breast with delight like its own!

What language can utter the feeling
Which rose, when in exile afar,
On the brow of a lonely hill kneeling,
I saw the brown heath growing there?

It was scattered and stunted, and told me
That soon even that would be gone:
It whispered, 'The grim walls enfold me,
I have bloomed in my last summer's sun.'

But not the loved music, whose waking
Makes the soul of the Swiss die away,
Has a spell more adored and heart-breaking
Than, for me, in that blighted heath lay.

The spirit which bent 'neath its power,
How it longed—how it burned to be free!
If I could have wept in that hour,
Those tears had been heaven to me.

Well—well; the sad minutes are moving,
Though loaded with trouble and pain;
And some time the loved and the loving
Shall meet on the mountains again!

Encouragement

I do not weep; I would not weep;
Our mother needs no tears:
Dry thine eyes, too; 'tis vain to keep
This causeless grief for years.

What though her brow be changed and cold,
Her sweet eyes closed for ever?
What though the stone-the darksome mould
Our mortal bodies sever?

What though her hand smooth ne'er again
Those silken locks of thine?
Nor, through long hours of future pain,
Her kind face o'er thee shine?

Remember still, she is not dead;
She sees us, sister, now;
Laid, where her angel spirit fled,
'Mid heath and frozen snow.

And from that world of heavenly light
Will she not always bend
To guide us in our lifetime's night,
And guard us to the end?

Thou knowest she will; and thou mayst mourn
That we are left below:
But not that she can ne'er return
To share our earthly woe.

Shall Earth No More Inspire Thee

Shall Earth no more inspire thee,
Thou lonely dreamer now ?
Since passion may not fire thee
Shall nature cease to bow ?

Thy mind is ever moving
In regions dark to thee;
Recall its useless roving -
Come back and dwell with me -

I know my mountain breezes
Enchant and soothe thee still -
I know my sunshine pleases
Despite thy wayward will -

When day with evening blending
Sinks from the summer sky,
I've seen thy spirit bending
In fond idolatry -

I've watched thee every hour -
I know my mighty sway -
I know my magic power
To drive thy griefs away -

Few hearts to mortal given
On earth so wildly pine
Yet none would ask a Heaven
More like this Earth than thine -

Then let my winds caress thee -
Thy comrade let me be -
Since nought beside can bless thee
Return and dwell with me -

Far Far Away Is Mirth Withdrawn

Far, far away is mirth withdrawn
'Tis three long hours before the morn
And I watch lonely, drearily -
So come thou shade commune with me

Deserted one ! thy corpse lies cold
And mingled with a foreign mould -
Year after year the grass grows green
Above the dust where thou hast been.

I will not name thy blighted name
Tarnished by unforgotten shame
Though not because my bosom torn
Joins the mad world in all its scorn -

Thy phantom face is dark with woe
Tears have left ghastly traces there,
Those ceaseless tears ! I wish their flow
Could quench thy wild despair.

They deluge my heart like the rain
On cursed Gomorrah's howling plain -
Yet when I hear thy foes deride
I must cling closely to thy side -

Our mutual foes - they will not rest
From trampling on thy buried breast -
Glutting there hatred with the doom
They picture thine, beyond the tomb -

But God is not like human kind
Man cannot read the Almighty mind
Vengeance will never torture they
Nor hunt thy soul eternally

Then do not in this night of grief
This time of over whelming fear
O do not think that God can leave
Forget, forsake, refuse to hear! -

What have I dreamt? He lies asleep
With whom my heart would vainly weep
He rests - and I endure the woe
That left his spirit long ago -

Long Neglect Has Worn Away

Long neglect has worn away
Half the sweet enchanting smile;
Time has turned the bloom to grey;
Mould and damp the face defile.

But that lock of silky hair,
Still beneath the picture twined,
Tells what once those features were,
Paints their image on the mind.

Fair the hand that traced that line,
"Dearest, ever deem me true";
Swiftly flew the fingers fine
When the pen that motto drew.

Spellbound

The night is darkening round me,
The wild winds coldly blow;
But a tyrant spell has bound me
And I cannot, cannot go.

The giant trees are bending
Their bare boughs weighed with snow.
And the storm is fast descending,
And yet I cannot go.

Clouds beyond clouds above me,
Wastes beyond wastes below;
But nothing drear can move me;
I will not, cannot go.

Ah! Why, Because The Dazzling Sun

Ah! why, because the dazzling sun
Restored my earth to joy
Have you departed, every one,
And left a desert sky?

All through the night, your glorious eyes
Were gazing down in mine,
And with a full heart's thankful sighs
I blessed that watch divine!

I was at peace, and drank your beams
As they were life to me
And revelled in my changeful dreams
Like petrel on the sea.

Thought followed thought—star followed star
Through boundless regions on,
While one sweet influence, near and far,
Thrilled through and proved us one.

Why did the morning rise to break
So great, so pure a spell,
And scorch with fire the tranquil cheek
Where your cool radiance fell?

Blood-red he rose, and arrow-straight,
His fierce beams struck my brow;
The soul of Nature sprang elate,
But mine sank sad and low!

My lids closed down—yet through their veil
I saw him blazing still;
And bathe in gold the misty dale,
And flash upon the hill.

I turned me to the pillow then
To call back Night, and see
Your worlds of solemn light, again
Throb with my heart and me!

It would not do—the pillow glowed
And glowed both roof and floor,
And birds sang loudly in the wood,
And fresh winds shook the door.

The curtains waved, the wakened flies
Were murmuring round my room,
Imprisoned there, till I should rise
And give them leave to roam.

O Stars and Dreams and Gentle Night;
O Night and Stars return!
And hide me from the hostile light
That does not warm, but burn—

That drains the blood of suffering men;
Drinks tears, instead of dew:
Let me sleep through his blinding reign,
And only wake with you!

Emily Bronte (1818 – 1848)

Portrait of Emily Bronte, by Patrick Branwell Bronte, 1833,
held at the National Portrait Gallery.

www.debbiebrewerauthor.com

Lightning Source UK Ltd.
Milton Keynes UK
UKHW020753230620
365445UK00010B/501